Good For Me
Grains and Cereals

Sally Hewitt

WAYLAND

Notes for Teachers and Parents

Good for Me is a series of books that looks at ways of helping children to develop a positive approach to eating. You can use the books to help children make healthy choices about what they eat and drink as an important part of a healthy lifestyle.

Look for grains and cereals when you go shopping.
- Look at the different types of grains and cereals in your local supermarket.
- Read the ingredients on packets and see if the food contains grains and cereals.
- Buy something new. Have fun preparing it and eating it together.

Talk about different food groups and how we need to eat a variety of food from each group every day.
- Grains and cereals are packed with vitamins, minerals and fibre.
- Talk about the ways vitamins, minerals and fibre help to keep us strong and healthy.

Talk about how we feel when we are healthy and the things we can do to help us to stay healthy.
- Eat food that is good for us.
- Drink plenty of water.
- Enjoy fresh air and exercise.
- Sleep well.

First published in 2007 by Wayland
Copyright © Wayland 2007
Wayland
338 Euston Road
London NW1 3BH

Wayland Australia
Hachette Children's Books
Level 17/207 Kent Street
Sydney NSW 2000

Produced by Tall Tree Ltd
Editor: Jon Richards
Designer: Ben Ruocco
Consultant: Sally Peters

British Library Cataloguing in Publication Data
Hewitt, Sally, 1949–
   Grains and cereals. – (Good for me!)
   1. Cereal as food – Juvenile literature 2. Carbohydrates in
   human nutrition – Juvenile literature 3. Health – Juvenile
   literature
   I. Title
   641.3'31

   ISBN-13: 9780750250023

Printed in China
Wayland is a division of Hachette Children's Books.

Picture credits:
Cover top Alamy/Ace Stock Limited, cover bottom Dreamstime.com/Nicolas Nadjar, 1 Dreamstime.com, 4 Corbis/Michael A. Keller, 5 Dreamstime.com/Alon Othnay, 6 Dreamstime.com, 7 Dreamstime.com, 8 Dreamstime.com, 9 Dreamstime.com/Myrthe Krook, 10 Dreamstime.com, 11 Dreamstime.com/Tobias Renschke, 12 courtesy John Deere, 13 Dreamstime.com, 14 Dreamstime.com/Nicolas Nadjar, 15 Alamy/Pixonnet.com, 16 Dreamstime.com/Michael Riccio, 17 Alamy/Diffused Productions, 18 Alamy/ImageState, 19 Corbis/Creasource, 20 top Dreamstime.com, bottom left Dreamstime.com/Will Hayward, bottom centre Digital Vision, bottom right Dreamstime.com, 21 top Dreamstime.com/Scott Rothstein top left Dreamstime.com, top centre Dreamstime.com/Paul Fairbrother, top right Dreamstime.com/Ewa Walicka, middle Dreamstime.com/Norman Chan, bottom left Dreamstime.com/Kheng Guan Toh, bottom centre Corbis/Envision, bottom right Alamy/Foodfolio, 23 Alamy/Michael Bluestone

Contents

Good for me

Everyone needs to eat food and drink water to live, grow and be healthy. All the food we eat comes from animals and plants. Grains and cereals are food from plants.

Breakfast cereal with milk is a healthy meal to start the day.

Cereals are grass plants, such as wheat, rice and corn. Farmers grow these in fields. The grain is part of the seed from these cereals. Grains are used to make meals. They are good for you!

Cereals need sunshine and rain to grow and **ripen**.

Healthy grains

Cereal grains are full of **vitamins** and **minerals**. Every part of your body needs vitamins and minerals to be healthy and to fight germs.

Grains give you energy for play and exercise.

Cereal grains are full of **fibre**, too. Fibre is important because it helps your body to get rid of unwanted food.

Lunch box

Mix cold pasta in a little olive oil and lemon juice. Add olives, salmon and chopped tomatoes to make a pasta salad.

Eating pasta will give you lots of energy because it is made from grains of wheat.

Seeds and grains

Grains are parts of the seeds that grow on cereal plants. Farmers collect the seeds and separate out the grains. These grains are then used to make different kinds of food.

Wheat seeds grow at the top of the wheat plant.

Sometimes, the cereal grains are crushed or **ground** to make flour. Flour from wheat is used to make bread and pasta.

These are wheat grains. The unwanted part of the seed, or **chaff**, has been removed.

Growing grains

All cereals need plenty of
sunshine to grow and ripen.
When wheat is ripe and golden,
it is ready to **harvest**.

These large machines spray water
onto cereals in dry countries.

Cereals also need water to grow. Rice needs lots of water to grow and rice plants are planted underwater.

Rice plants grow in flooded fields called **paddies**.

Lunch box

Mix cooked brown rice with chopped peppers, apple and raisins to make a tasty rice salad.

Harvesting and milling

At harvest time, a machine called a **combine harvester** cuts the wheat and separates the grain from the **stalks**.

The combine harvester empties the wheat grains into a waiting tractor.

The wheat grains are taken to a **mill** and ground into flour. The grains are still covered by an outer layer. Brown flour is made by grinding the whole grain, including the grain's outside covering.

White flour is made from grains that have had their covering taken off.

Lunch box

Try eating dark crispbread that is made from whole grains with their outside covering.

Eating bread

Many different grains are used to make bread. Rye makes dark, heavy bread. Millet is used to make flat bread called chapatti. **Baguettes** are made with white wheat flour.

Bread contains lots of fibre which helps our bodies get rid of unwanted food.

Bread is made from flour, water and **yeast**. Yeast makes this bread mixture rise. Flat bread is made without yeast. The mixture is put in the oven to bake.

Lunch box

Try different kinds of bread for lunch such as brown rolls, pitta bread or make a wrap using flat bread.

Bread mixture is pushed and squeezed before it is put in the oven. This is called kneading.

Storing grains

Dried pasta, rice and flour should be kept in a dry place, such as a sealed jar. This will stop them from getting wet and going bad.

Long spaghetti can be stored in a tall glass jar to keep it dry.

Rice grains and dried pasta made from wheat flour may last for up to a year. Fresh pasta should be kept in a fridge and eaten within a week of buying it.

Lunch box

Try eating a rice cake spread with hummus for a healthy snack.

Bread can be stored in a large tin with a lid to keep it fresh for about five days.

Cooking grains

You can cook grains. Cooked rice can be mixed with other foods, including vegetables, fish and meat. Rice is also served with many dishes, such as curries.

Dried rice grains are cooked in boiling water to make them soft.

Flour from grains is used to make bread, pasta and cakes. It is used to thicken sauces, soups and stews. There are thousands of different recipes from all over the world that use flour.

Spaghetti is a type of pasta. Pasta is made using flour, eggs and water.

Lunch box

Couscous is made from wheat flour. Mix some cold couscous with chopped vegetables and olive oil for your lunch.

19

Food chart

Here are some examples of dishes that can be made using three types of cereal grain. Have you tried any of these?

Wheat

Noodles

Bread

Pancakes

Corn

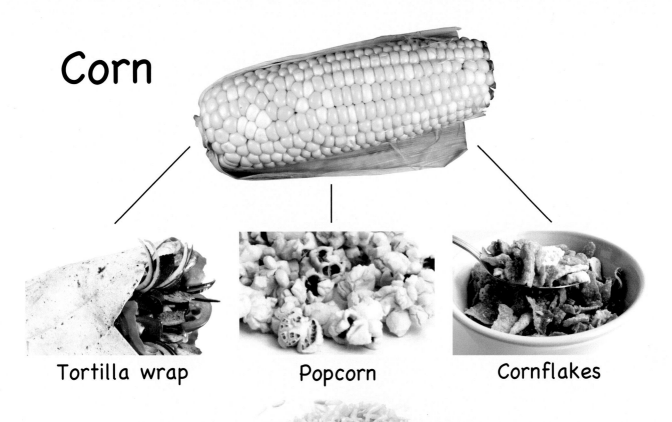

Tortilla wrap

Popcorn

Cornflakes

Rice

Rice and peas

Rice cakes

Rice pudding

A balanced diet

This chart shows you how much you can eat of each food group. The larger the area on the chart, the more of that food group you can eat. For example, you can eat a lot of fruit and vegetables, but only a little oil and sweets. Drink plenty of water every day, too.

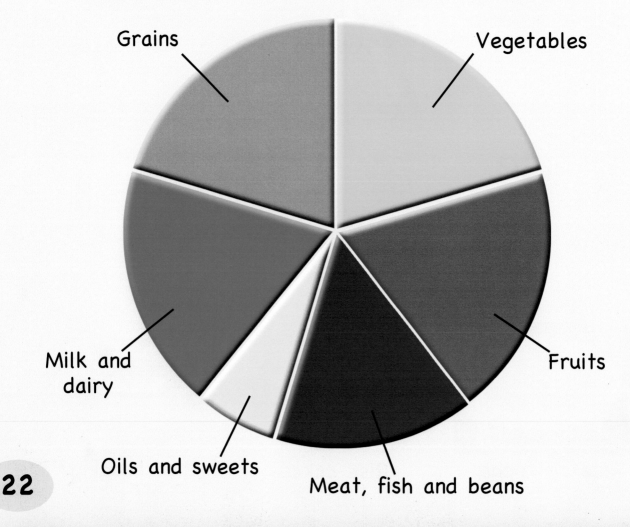

Grains

Vegetables

Milk and dairy

Fruits

Oils and sweets

Meat, fish and beans

Our bodies also need exercise to stay healthy. You should spend at least 20 minutes exercising every day so that your body stays fit and healthy.

Running exercises your leg muscles and keeps your heart healthy.

Glossary

Baguettes Long sticks of bread.

Chaff The unwanted part of a cereal seed.

Combine harvester A machine that harvests cereals and separates the grain from the plant.

Fibre The rough part of grains.

Ground When something is crushed.

Harvest Collecting the seeds of cereal plants.

Mill Where grains are crushed into flour.

Minerals Important substances found in food. For example, iron keeps your heart healthy.

Paddies Flooded fields where rice plants grow.

Ripen When something becomes ready to eat.

Stalks The upright parts of plants.

Vitamins Important substances found in food. For example, vitamin D gives you strong bones.

Yeast A type of fungus that is used in the baking of bread.

Index